PRIMARY SOURCES TEACHING KIT

Immigration

by Karen Baicker

SCHOLASTIC
PROFESSIONALBOOKS

New York • Toronto • London • Auckland • Sydney
Mexico City • New Delhi • Hong Kong • Buenos Aires

for Adria McCuaig

COVER DOCUMENTS: **Library of Congress:** Passport; Immigrants disembarking; Immigrant family portrait; **North Wind Picture Archive:** Harper's Weekly cartoon

INTERIOR DOCUMENTS: **AMI—National Park Service, Department of Interior:** 24, 27; **AP/Wide World Photos:** 41; **Bettman/Corbis:** 32; **Corbis:** 19; **The Estate of Irving Berlin:** 37; **Library of Congress:** 23; 26; 30 (top left, bottom); 33 (top, bottom); 34 (top) [LC-USZ62-16348]; 34 (bottom); **The Granger Collection,** New York, NY: 20; 32; **Getty Images:** 22; **Herbert Block:** 29 (originally printed in *The Washington Post*, 1946); **Minnesota Historical Society:** 21; **National Archives:** 31; 35 (top); **National Geographic Image Collection**: 35 (bottom) [NGM 1981/04351A]; 36 [NGM 1981/04351];**Reuters New Media/Corbis:** 40 (top); **Steve Rubin/The Image Works:** 40 (bottom); **UPI/Corbis:** 38;

Edited by Sean Price
Picture research by Dwayne Howard
Cover design by Norma Ortiz
Interior design and illustrations by Melinda Belter
ISBN 0-590-37866-X

Contents

INTRODUCTION

Using Primary Sources in the Classroom

Since its birth, the United States has welcomed immigrants to its borders. Yet discussion about U.S. immigration has often been heated, fueled by controversy. The issues that confront us today—how to establish quotas, determining who is and isn't offered citizenship, how to handle illegal immigrants, and so on—are the same ones that have sparked debate for over two hundred years. The documents in this collection give a sense of the push-and-pull that continues to characterize our country's relationship to immigrants.

Primary sources offer a wealth of other benefits for your students as well. Textbooks often present a single interpretation of events; primary sources compel the reader to supply his own interpretation. A thoughtful analysis of primary sources requires both basic and advanced critical thinking skills: determining point of view; evaluating bias; classification; comparing and contrasting; reading for detail.

Primary sources can also help students recognize that the artifacts of our contemporary lives—a ticket stub, a school report card, a yearbook—may one day be fodder for future historians.

One of the most important steps is to help students understand the difference between primary and secondary sources. Share the chart below to demonstrate the categories to your class.

MATERIAL	DEFINITION	EXAMPLES
Primary Sources	Documents created during or immediately following the event they describe, by people who had firsthand knowledge of the event	Letters, diaries, photographs, artifacts, newspaper articles, paintings
Secondary Sources	Documents created by people who were not present at the event they describe	History books, biographies, newspaper articles

Keep a folder handy with copies of the Primary Source Evaluation Form on page 15. Encourage students to complete this reproducible as they study each document in this book. Eventually, that kind of analysis will be automatic for your students as they encounter primary sources in their future studies.

Using the Internet to Find Primary Sources

The Internet can be an amazing tool for finding primary sources. Just remind your students that extra care has to be taken in verifying that the source is reliable. Here are a few outstanding sites for using primary sources in the classroom:

Library of Congress: **http://www.loc.gov**

National Archives Records Administration: **http://www.nara.gov**

Internet Archive of Texts and Documents: **http://history.hanover.edu/texts.htm**

The American Immigration Home Page: **http://www.bergen.org/AAST/Projects/Immigration/**

The official web site of Ellis Island: **http://www.ellisisland.org**

Ask your students to find other great sites for primary sources and create their own list. Keep a running list handy, posted near a computer terminal.

Background on Immigration (1790–2001)

It is often said that the United States is a nation of immigrants. The first of them were ancient peoples from Asia. About 12,000 years ago, they crossed a land bridge (which no longer exists) between Siberia and Alaska. Today's Native Americans are descended from these people.

The European discovery of the New World in 1492 by Christopher Columbus triggered a fresh influx of immigrants. Most European settlers came willingly, trying to strike it rich or start a new life. However, others came in chains as convicts. Millions of Africans were also brought in chains as unwilling slaves. Packed in slave ships, many died during the horrible journey.

Truly massive immigration did not take place until the early 1800s. Immigrants were pushed by calamities in Europe like the Irish potato famine. They were also pulled by events like the 1849 discovery of gold in California. The gold rush prompted immigration from Asia as well as Europe. For the first time large numbers of Chinese people lived side-by-side by large numbers of English, French, and other Europeans.

Americans are most familiar with the wave of immigration that took place between 1880 and 1920. At least 23 million new arrivals turned up on America's doorstep, most of them from Europe. Many were processed through Ellis Island and were greeted by the Statue of Liberty. This wave of immigration died out in part because of World War I. Around that time, an anti-immigrant backlash led to new quotas on immigration.

Less-restrictive immigration laws passed in the 1960s renewed the surge in immigrants to the U.S. For the first time, though, they were not predominantly European. They came from Asia, Africa, South America, Mexico, and Central America. The terrorist attacks of 9/11 have heralded a new wave of policies and attitudes toward immigrants. History shows us that the current reactions are part of the ongoing pendulum swing of our nation's views of newcomers. As in the past, immigrants will continue to come here looking for a fresh start, and will continue to reshape our society.

About this Book

Immigration has always been a hot topic in the United States, so the subject is well documented. Firsthand accounts including letters, photos, and interviews help bring the immigrant experience alive for your students.

This book does not focus on the first immigrants: Native Americans, European colonists, and African slaves. Instead, it picks up the story in the early 1800s when immigration to the U.S. hit flood stage. If possible, review some basic background about the earliest immigrants with your students (see above).

Students studying any firsthand sources on immigration need context. They also need to be engaged with critical viewing and thinking activities. Your classes can prepare for a discussion about any of the documents in this collection by studying them and completing the reproducible Evaluate That Document! (page 17). Feel free to copy this form as you need it.

The Teaching Notes section provides background information and teaching suggestions for each document. Reproducible pages for the activity suggestions can be found at the back of the book.

Some of the documents, such as handwritten letters, are difficult to read in their original form. They have been typeset to make them accessible. All the documents included here should help your students understand one of the greatest forces shaping the United States.

Immigration Time Line

(1790–2001)

1790 The Naturalization Act restricts citizenship to "free white persons" who live in the U.S. for five years and renounce their previous citizenship.

1808 The legal importation of African slaves is banned. However, illegal importation continues until the Civil War.

1840 –1850 A decade of turmoil in Europe prompts mass immigration to the U.S. Irish flee the potato famine. Germans flee crop failures and a failed revolution. Others flee displacement caused by the Industrial Revolution.

1848 The California gold rush prompts greater westward movement and a surge in immigration.

1861 The American Civil War begins. Immigration decreases until the war ends in 1865.

1862 Homestead Act provides free land in the Midwest to settlers.

1868 The first Japanese laborers arrive in Hawaii. Some migrate to Southern California.

1870 A new naturalization law restricts citizenship to people of European and African descent. Asians are excluded.

1882 The Chinese Exclusion Act becomes one of the first major restrictions on immigration to the United States.

1885 The Statue of Liberty, a gift from France, is erected in New York harbor.

1891 Congress establishes the Bureau of Immigration within the Treasury Department.

1892 Ellis Island opens, becoming the main doorway for legal immigrants to enter the United States.

1907 An informal agreement between the U.S. and Japan excludes Japanese laborers from the U.S. mainland, though they may immigrate to Hawaii. Also, a new law says that any American woman marrying a foreign national loses her citizenship.

1910 Angel Island Immigration Station begins operation near San Francisco.

1918 New quota systems favor British and Northern European immigrants.

1924 The Immigration Act of 1924 greatly limits the number of immigrants. The new laws, followed by the Great Depression in the 1930s, cause a sharp decline in immigration rates. Almost all immigrants from Asia are officially excluded.

1940 The Chinese Exclusion Act is repealed.

1948 The Displaced Persons Act allows immigration of more than 395,000 refugees from war-torn European nations.

1952 Immigration and Nationality Act (McCarran-Walter Act) places further restrictions on immigration. The total quota for Europe is 149,667, compared with 2,990 for Asia and 1,400 for Africa.

1965 The Immigration Act of 1965 changes the quota system. This allows greater immigration from all countries, not just those in Europe.

1980 The Refugee Act allows 10 million permanent immigrants to be admitted legally. It is enacted in response to the plight of boat people fleeing Vietnam.

1986 The Immigration Reform and Control Act is passed, granting amnesty to illegal immigrants.

1990 Immigration Act of 1990 increases the number of immigrants allowed into the U.S.

1996 The Immigration and Welfare Reform Act strengthens border enforcement. It also reduces many of the rights, protections, and benefits previously granted to immigrants.

2001 USA PATRIOT Act is enacted in response to September 11. The legislation grants the government more powers to investigate, detain, and deport immigrants.

THE FIRST GREAT WAVE

The Potato Famine: 1845

Use with pages 18–19.

BACKGROUND

From 1815 to 1860 more Irish came to America than any other group of immigrants. At the time, Protestant Great Britain ruled over Roman Catholic Ireland. Protestant landlords oversaw tenant farms worked by Catholic laborers. Most landlords treated tenants poorly, often evicting them simply to consolidate their farm holdings and using the excuse that the tenants could not pay the high rents they set. Though Ireland's economic fortunes waxed and waned, there remained widespread resentment among Catholics toward the wealthier Protestants. Likewise, most Protestants looked down on the poorer Catholics. This harsh treatment of the Catholics caused thousands to emigrate to the U.S.

By 1845, 1.5 million of Ireland's 8.5 million people were totally dependent upon one crop—the potato. Another 3 million were mostly dependent upon it. Almost all these people were poor farmers and rural laborers. Adult males might eat up to 14 pounds of potatoes a day. Then a potato blight, or fungus, spread from the eastern U.S. to Ireland and the rest of Europe. Whole fields of potatoes became inedible. From 1845 to 1860, out-and-out starvation caused by the blight prompted a mass exodus from Ireland. Over a million came to the United States, driven by the famine and by eviction from big landowners.

The photograph shows a group of Irish men using a battering ram to evict a family from their cottage. In the wood engraving, Irish emigrants are receiving the priest's blessing before leaving for America. The trip these evicted emigrants were about to make would be dangerous and take weeks. Poor, ignorant people were packed on board unseaworthy vessels soon known as "coffin ships." Two brief accounts describe some of the hardships aboard these ships. The first is by Robert Whyte, a middle-class Irish emigrant. The second is by Vere Foster, a British social reformer.

Those who survived the voyage often faced hostility and discrimination in the U.S. Many Americans were biased against the Irish because they were poor, Catholic, and would often work for low wages. Many Irish immigrants coming off the boat were met by con men trying to sweet-talk or rob them of their last possessions. However, numerous organizations, such as the Irish Emigrant Society, attempted to help. They offered a sense of community and practical assistance. The Irish, unlike the numerous German-speaking emigrants of the time, generally stayed in the Eastern cities and helped build much of America's early transportation infrastructure.

TEACHING SUGGESTIONS

➡ Distribute copies of the Evaluate That Document! form (page 17). Have students study the drawing, photograph, and excerpts. Discuss the ways that each medium provides information in a different way. For example, the photograph shows how real and how brutal the process could be. The words provide a window into real people's thoughts. Which format do the students find most powerful, and why?

➡ Let students know that the wood engraving is from an English newspaper printed in 1851. How might this perspective come through in the illustration? What might an Irish artist have depicted differently?

➡ Have your students read the two brief passages about traveling on a "coffin ship." What problems do these accounts relate? What other problems do they hint at? What similarities do your students see in the two stories?

➡ In the account by Robert Whyte, the passengers give up after a show of force by the captain. Yet Whyte says the men could easily have gotten what they wanted. Ask your students why they might have hesitated. Remind them of the oppression that Irish people were used to back home.

➡ Distribute copies of the Immigration Map on page 45. Have students trace the route from Ireland to the United States. You may also want to have them study the Immigration Tides graph on page 27. Have them find the peak on the graph that corresponds to the potato famine.

Lure of the Land: mid- to late 1800s

Use with pages 20–21.

BACKGROUND

In the 1800s, the prospect of owning large tracts of arable land lured many Europeans with agricultural backgrounds. Especially after Congress passed the Homestead Act in 1862, settlers, both native and foreign, streamed westward to take advantage of offers of free or practically free land. (The Homestead Act allowed for settlers to claim 160 acres in exchange for five years' worth of farming the land.) States and territories west of the Mississippi advertised to attract settlers, including in western European newspapers, which directly targeted prospective immigrants.

The American Land Company broadside, or advertisement, encourages immigrants to purchase government lands in California. It uses the image of the cornucopia and the promise of a "climate for health and wealth" to entice prospective buyers.

"Where to Emigrate and Why" is a frontispiece, a page at the beginning of a book, from a guide for emigrants. The guide was widely distributed in Europe. At the top of the page, a plot of untended land is shown. The bottom image depicts the land bearing the fruits of immigrant labor.

TEACHING SUGGESTIONS

➡ Distribute copies of Evaluate That Document! (page 17) and ask students to identify the types of documents shown on this page. One is a poster and one is a frontispiece. Help students to understand these terms. How might that format influence students' reading of the document?

➡ Ask students what the words and picture on the broadside promise about life in California. Discuss why these inducements might have drawn settlers. Then ask students to make their own broadsides encouraging people to move to frontier land in the mid-1800s.

➡ Ask students to study the two images on the "Where to Emigrate and Why" document. What are the differences between the two scenes? What point is made by the illustration?

The Gold Rush: 1849

Use with page 22.

BACKGROUND

The discovery of gold near Sutter's Mill in California set off a worldwide stampede. About 85,000 men descended on California's gold fields, and about 23,000 of them were not Americans. One Californian said the mines "are loaded to the muzzle with vagabonds from every quarter of the globe, scoundrels from nowhere .... accomplished gentlemen from Europe, interlopers from Lima and Chile, Mexican thieves, [and] gamblers of no particular spot . . . ."

The 49ers—named for a peak year of "gold rush fever," 1849—had a pecking order. White Americans were at the top; Mexicans and Chinese were at the bottom. But all of them shared gold fever. In a few years, the gold fields played out and most foreigners moved on. But they often stayed in the United States to do other work. At the beginning of the gold rush, only a handful of Chinese immigrants could be found in all of California. In a few short years, more than 20,000 of them lived there. The photograph shows Chinese workers panning for gold. "Placers" shoveled sand from the bottom of a stream, painstakingly sifting for glints of gold. Accompanying the photograph are the words of a man named Huie Kin, recollecting his decision to leave China in 1865, at age 14. During this period in Chinese history, the United States was often referred to as "Gam Saan," which means Golden Mountain. Kin's memoirs provide proof of the idea that Asians too, had visions of America as a place where people could get rich overnight. The last paragraph also provides insight into the grim hardship of daily life in rural China at that time. Poverty, famine, natural disasters, political upheaval, civil wars, and foreign invasions provided real impetus for people to leave.

TEACHING SUGGESTIONS

➡ Analyze the photograph of the miners, using the Evaluate That Document! form. What can students tell about the conditions of miners in California during the gold rush? What can they tell by the miners' dress?

➡ Read aloud the quote from the background section and have students compare the perspective with Huie Kin's words.

➡ Explain to students that non-European immigrants faced tremendous discrimination among gold miners. Why do they think that happened?

The Magic Washer: 1886

Use with page 23.

BACKGROUND

Most immigrant groups met with some kind of discrimination. Except for enslaved Africans, though, none endured more vicious discrimination than the Chinese did. Language and custom separated them almost completely from other immigrants.

In the 1870s, the slogan, "The Chinese must go!" became a rallying cry for American workers who were now worried about competition for jobs during harder economic times. The Chinese were targeted in part because they were famously thrifty, hard-working, and willing to accept low wages. Discriminatory cartoons highlighted those physical features, religions, and ways of dressing that distinguished the Chinese from other immigrants.

This advertisement for "Magic Washer," a clothes washing product, shows Uncle Sam kicking a "Chinaman" out. It suggests that the Chinese, who often worked in the laundry business, would no longer be needed.

By 1880 about 100,000 Chinese lived in the U.S., mostly in California. They became the first immigrant group in U.S. history to be almost completely barred from entering the country when Congress passed the Chinese Exclusion Act of 1882. The act was not repealed until 1943, when Chinese refugees were fleeing their country during World War II.

TEACHING SUGGESTIONS

➡ Have students identify this document as an advertisement, and evaluate its message using the Evaluate That Document! form (page 17). What is the advertisement trying to sell?

➡ Discuss with students what Uncle Sam is shown doing in the ad? What message is it trying to convey?

➡ How might the Magic Washer have had an influence on Chinese immigrants?

➡ Distribute the Immigration Map on page 45 and ask students to locate China and San Francisco on the map. Students might then investigate travel routes of Chinese immigrants in the 1800s and the distances they traveled.

America Fever: 1870s–1880s

Use with pages 24–25.

BACKGROUND

This portrait shows a Scandinavian immigrant family, standing outside their home in Minnesota, around the late 1800s. Many people from Norway, Sweden, Finland, and Denmark journeyed to this part of the country, settling in to lead farming lives in the harsh environment. Most had been farmers in their home countries.

Accompanying the photograph are the recollections of Andreas Ueland, a Norwegian immigrant to Minnesota in 1871. The two paragraphs are excerpted from his book As a Newcomer. *The book is a highly readable and engaging account of the young man's travels to and life in the United States. The excerpt speaks of his motivation for leaving Norway—his case of "America fever." Of course, Ueland was not alone in using the term "America fever." Many people used it to describe the widespread desire of people to come to this country.*

Also included is a letter from C.F. Carlsson. He wrote from Clarksville, Nebraska, to his ancestral home in Dalarna, Sweden, about the abundance he found in the Great Plains. Though many of the immigrant documents show that life was not as golden as immigrants imagined, this letter reveals the optimism and enthusiasm characterized many immigrants' experiences.

TEACHING SUGGESTIONS

➡ Distribute copies of the Evaluate That Document! form and have students study the photographs and two excerpts. What do the documents say about immigrants from Scandinavia? Where did they like to settle? What were they looking for in the U.S.?

➡ Letters such as this helped spur greater immigration. Many settled near other immigrants from the same country, creating ethnic communities that still exist today. How might these communities have helped immigrants adjust to their new lives?

- Distribute the Immigration Map (page 45) and have students locate the country Carlsson came from and the state in which he lived.

- Discuss the Homestead Act of 1862 and how it influenced the westward movement of immigrants.

"Only an Emigrant": 1879

Use with page 26.

BACKGROUND

The lyrics shown on this document come from a simple song entitled "Only an Emigrant," written by Charles Baker in 1879. It suggests the spirit of thousands of eager newcomers, who yearned for their own little place on the American prairie, and were truly willing, eager, and able to work hard to make their dreams come true. Such people helped transform the prairies into some of the most productive agricultural land in the world.

TEACHING SUGGESTIONS

- Another verse from the same song reads:

  Nobody cares for my grief or distress,
  Friendless am I in the world today…

  Discuss the different sentiment in the two verses, using the Evaluate That Document! form (page 17).

- Another song from emigrants in Wisconsin reflects back on life before America:

  Since times are so hard, I've thought, my true heart,
  Of leaving my oxen, my plough and my cart,
  And away to Wisconsin, a journey we'd go
  To double our fortune as other folks do,
  While here I must labor each day in the field,
  And the winter consumes all the summer doth yield.

  Ask students to write their own verses about life in the west for immigrants. They may want to research the midwest American tall-tale hero Febold Feboldson.

THE SECOND GREAT WAVE

Immigration Tides: 1800–2000

Use with page 27.

BACKGROUND

Immigration is often said to have happened in waves. This document demonstrates that graphically, showing the ups and downs of legal immigration from 1800 to 2000. The period from 1880 to 1924 is considered the time of the "second great wave," when as many as 20 million people managed to make their way to the shores of America. The busiest year was 1907, when more than 1 million people arrived. A huge portion of these people came from southern and eastern Europe this time, unlike in the past—places like Italy, Hungary, Poland, and Russia. People of many religions were represented, including large numbers of Jews, who often fled Europe to escape persecution and violence.

The 1906 photograph gives another view of the scope of these numbers, in the form of one ship's deck full of immigrants. Journeys from Europe to New York generally took about two weeks and poorer passengers—the majority—traveled in steerage quarters below deck.

TEACHING SUGGESTIONS

- Discuss the different view of the numbers afforded by the graph and the photograph. Which document provides a more powerful account of the scope of immigration during the Second Great Wave? Distribute copies of the Evaluate That Document! form and ask students to record their interpretations.

- To simulate the crowded conditions of the ship, mark off an area in the classroom to represent the ship deck. Have students "board the deck," one at a time, until the space appears to be as crowded as the picture shown. Ask students to imagine what it might have been like to travel in such crowded conditions overseas to a foreign country. They can use the glossary and journal reproducibles (pages 46 and 47) to write several diary entries about the trip to America.

- Ask students to look at the graph and correlate the peaks and lows with different events in history. You can refer to the Time Line on page 6 to help with this activity. For example, what international events might have caused the great jump from the 1890s to the 1900s? What might have caused the decrease in immigration in the 1930s?

- Distribute copies of the Immigration Map (page 45) and help students identify the countries from which major waves of immigrants came.

- Incorporate some math activities using the immigration graphs. Some sample questions might include, *What year saw the biggest jump? What was the average change over a certain time period?* You can find more print-ready immigration statistics and graphs at the Scholastic.com teacher page: Immigration, Stories of Yesterday and Today at **http://teacher.scholastic.com/ immigrant/facts.htm**.

The Statue of Liberty: 1884

Use with pages 28–29.

BACKGROUND

Immigrants entering New York harbor were often stirred by their first look at the Statue of Liberty. The statue was created by Auguste Bartholdi and given as a gift to the United States from France in 1884. The statue was and remains a symbol of liberty and opportunity. The wood engraving, print-ed in Frank Leslie's Illustrated Newspaper *in July, 1887, shows people on board a crowded boat, talk-ing and pointing toward the statue as they approach their new home. The drawing is accompanied by a quote from Elizabeth Phillips, an Irish immigrant. She describes the animated reaction of fellow pas-sengers spotting the Statue of Liberty.*

Also included is a copy of Emma Lazarus' sonnet "The New Colossus." It is inscribed on a plaque on the statue's pedestal. Lazarus composed the poem in 1883, and it was read aloud for the first time that year at a Statue of Liberty fund raiser. The poem's last five lines are well known.

The 1946 cartoon, "What Happened To The One We Used To Have?" is a commentary on policies that did not welcome immigrants. Later, in 1965, in response to President Lyndon B. Johnson signed an immigration act abolishing quotas set for individual countries. Instead, it set a maximum number of immigrants in total to be accepted each year.

Recently, stricter policies toward immigration have been enacted, in part as a response to 9/11. Some historical background may help students to see these shifts as part of a continuing push-and-pull of national feelings towards immigration. Use the Time Line on page 6 and the Immigration Tides graph on page 27 to discuss the changing policies and views.

TEACHING SUGGESTIONS

- Have students use the Evaluate that Document! form (page 17) to analyze the drawing from *Leslie's Weekly.* Then have them read Phillips' quote. Discuss why immigrants might have been so awed by the statue? Remind students that many came from poor backgrounds or from repressive countries.

- Read aloud or conduct a choral reading of the poem by Emma Lazarus. Do students agree with its sentiments? Do they think the U.S. should still be "the Mother of Exiles"? Point out that many Americans at the time did not agree with Lazarus. Their attitudes eventually led to tighter immigration laws. Ask students to discuss whether they think immigration should be restricted today. How should quotas be determined?

- Have students study the 1946 cartoon and dis-cuss the point of view it represents. Ask students if they think the cartoon could represent policies and feelings toward immigrants today. Challenge them to draw a cartoon of the Statue of Liberty that represents a current point of view.

Ellis Island: 1892–1954

Use with pages 30–31.

BACKGROUND

Between 1892 and 1954, more than 12 million immigrants arrived at Ellis Island, which lies just off the southern tip of Manhattan. On busy days, at least 5,000 people were processed there. It's esti-mated that 40 percent of all Americans can trace their ancestry to someone who passed though Ellis Island.

The first photograph on page 30 shows the island station where prospective immigrants were examined and processed before they were allowed to set foot on the mainland. Once inside Ellis Island's facilities, new arrivals were shuffled into various lines and waiting areas, marked

off by wire fences. Immigration officials watched for disqualifying signs of mental or physical illness, marked anyone they felt needed further examination, and sent them off to other waiting areas. About 20 percent of prospective immigrants endured extra tests or questioning and about 2 percent had to return to their country of origin during the peak years.

The photo at the bottom of the page shows a man with chalk marks on his right shoulder undergoing an eye examination. Family members look on and other prospective immigrants sit waiting to move to the next stage of processing. If one family member did not qualify to enter the country, his or her family had to make an agonizing decision: Should the rejected person return alone to the old country or should the whole family go back?

Those arrivals who passed their examinations and had all their paperwork in order—including a stamped passport, such as the 1916 passport of a Greek immigrant shown on this page—headed by boat to Manhattan where many stayed and many boarded trains to reach points further afield.

The document on page 31 is a questionnaire used by the Cunard Line to prescreen immigrants. Steamship lines like the Cunard tried to weed out unacceptable immigrants before they left the old country. Anyone rejected had to be returned at the company's expense. Special attention should be paid to questions 17–22. If an immigrant admitted to being either a polygamist or an anarchist, deportation was assured. Additionally, immigration officials wanted to make sure potential immigrants would not become wards of the state. So an immigrant who lined up work in the U.S. ahead of time (as suggested in question 20) boosted his or her chances of being admitted.

TEACHING SUGGESTIONS

➡ Ask your students to use the Evaluate that Document! form (page 17) to study the test given by the Cunard Line. Have students read the Cunard Line's questionnaire. Steamship lines prescreened immigrants in their host countries because anyone who was rejected at Ellis Island had to go back at the expense of the company. Have students consider why the government might have asked these questions and why this form might have been intimidating to immigrants?

➡ Ask students to study all the documents and determine what types of information U.S. immigration officials were looking for. Have them identify the X and other chalk marks on the right shoulder of the man in the eye examination photo and look carefully at the expressions of the on-looking family and the other waiting immigrants. Discuss what the photograph tells them about the experiences of these new arrivals at Ellis Island.

Angel Island: 1910–1940

Use with page 32.

BACKGROUND

In 1910, Angel Island immigration station opened just outside San Francisco. It was billed as "the Ellis Island of the west." But it was more of a holding cell for Asian immigrants than a processing center.

Angel Island's chief job was to enforce the Chinese Exclusion Act of 1882 and keep out Chinese immigrants. But its role was not limited to the Chinese. In 1907, the U.S. and Japan struck an agreement limiting Japanese immigration. The U.S. agreed to not restrict Japanese immigration as long as Japan refused to issue passports to Japanese laborers bound for the continental U.S. Those laborers could travel to Hawaii but were barred from coming to the mainland.

To get around the Exclusion Act, many Chinese bought false papers claiming that they were the son or daughter of a Chinese-American citizen. Since official birth records were scanty at the time, U.S. immigration officials detained each new arrival and put him through a tough interview process. They were grilled on their home village, their ancestors, their parents, and anything else officials could think of to trip up the prospective immigrant. Most Angel Island detentions lasted for two or three weeks. Some lasted for months. A few stretched as long as two years.

Angel Island closed in 1940 after a fire destroyed the administration building (the Exclusion Act was finally repealed three years later). During its 30-year career, about 175,000 Chinese immigrants arrived there. Other immigrants coming from the Pacific also landed there, including Filipinos, Koreans, and Russians. Since the agreement with Japan allowed the wives of Japanese-Americans to come, many Japanese emigrants arranged marriages with women back in Japan by exchanging photographs with them. Between 6,000 and 19,000 Japanese "picture brides" were processed at Angel Island.

While detained on Angel Island, many Chinese immigrants expressed their hopes and fears in poetry on the wooden walls of their barracks. These poems were almost destroyed 1970 when the barracks was scheduled to be torn down. However, an alert park ranger saw the poems and began an effort to preserve Angel Island. The effort paid off and today Angel Island is a popular tourist site.

TEACHING SUGGESTIONS

➡ The poems written on the barracks walls were a way for the Chinese detainees to express their anger, frustration, and, despite these emotions, their hopes. Distribute copies of Evaluate That Document! (page 17) and discuss the feelings expressed in these poems.

➡ Have students study the photograph of boys waiting to be examined at Angel Island. Distribute the Immigration Journal (page 47), and ask students to write a poem from the point of view of one of the boys. Discuss how reading these poems on a barracks wall might have a different feeling than reading them on paper.

➡ Ask students to compare and contrast the two immigration stations, Ellis Island and Angel Island.

LIFE IN AMERICA

At Home, at Work, at Play: early 1900s

Use with pages 33–34.

BACKGROUND

Life was usually tough for newly arrived immigrants. In New York and other big east coast cities, the streets were teeming with unskilled workers who competed for jobs. Many families took in piecework so that the whole family could contribute to making ends meet, as shown by the photo of the immigrant family sewing at home on page 33. The second photo of street vendors selling fish offers a view of

the type of job available to new arrivals with limited English skills and little formal education at the beginning of the twentieth century. Others were forced into harsh conditions in big factories or tiny "sweatshops" where they were underpaid and had little recourse to fair labor standards.

The photographs on page 34 highlight the conditions of tenement living. Most immigrants with little money lived in crowded tenement housing. Tenements were buildings crammed with as many people as possible—each floor was divided into several apartments and each apartment in turn was divided into several smaller rooms. Sometimes people found ways to make use of spaces that weren't authorized living spaces, as the 1890 photo of a New York City tenement interior shows. There was seldom running water and often a whole building shared one or two outdoor privies. Immigrant children often had to use the streets for their entertainment and exercise. The last photo shows kids improvising a baseball game in a crowded Boston alley.

TEACHING SUGGESTIONS

➡ Distribute copies of Evaluate That Document! Have your students study these photos. Ask them what they think is happening. Point out the crowded, often dirty conditions that most immigrants lived in. Also explain the grueling working conditions that most immigrants had to endure.

➡ Jacob Riis and Lewis Hine were two immigrants who were concerned with the plight of immigrants, especially children. They used their skills as writers and photographers to depict the conditions of immigrant life. Ask students to pretend they are newspaper reporters interviewing Riis and Hine in the late 1800s. What did they discover about immigrant life? Why did Riis and Hine spend so much time recording the lives of immigrants? Students can learn more about the work of Riis and Hine in the book *Immigrant Kids* by Russell Freedman (EP Dutton, 1980).

➡ New York City has a Tenement Museum on the Lower East Side: **http://www.tenement.org/**. Students can visit their Web site and take a virtual tour. Ask students to write a script for a tour guide for the Tenement Museum.

Becoming an American: early 1900s

Use with pages 35–36.

BACKGROUND

Part of every immigrant's passage into permanent residency in the United States is the process of "Americanization." Many newcomers in the early 1900s lived in culturally homogeneous neighborhoods, which postponed their total immersion into the mainstream culture. Still, most learned English and sent their children to local public schools, making it inevitable that the next generation would be more assimilated. The broadside on page 35 prods adult arrivals to come to school so that they can become more American in language, dress, and attitude. The photo shows adults learning English in a classroom, and simultaneously being given a lesson in good grooming. Another photograph shows a teacher "preparing breakfast." The song lyrics, "Don't Bite the Hand That's Feeding You," became a kind of anthem aimed at immigrants around the beginning of World War I.

TEACHING SUGGESTIONS

➡ The process of "becoming American" and assimilating, while retaining parts of one's old culture, is one of the essential dynamics of immigration. By the turn of the century, there was a tremendous pressure to be American. Yet many people longed to retain their old customs, and bonded with other immigrants from their old country in their new community. Distribute copies of Evaluate That Document! (page 17) and discuss the views toward Americanization shown with each of the documents in this section.

➡ Lyrics and mottos such as "Don't Bite The Hand That's Feeding You" and "Love It or Leave It" (a more contemporary motto) represent views that have been widely held by Americans at points in our history. Ask students to discuss what these phrases suggest. Do they agree with them?

➡ Melting pot. Mosaic. Quilt. Tossed Salad. Many images have been used to describe the mix of different cultures that comprise our population. Ask students to discuss which metaphor— or perhaps another—best describes our population.

"God Bless America": 1938

Use with page 37.

BACKGROUND

Irving Berlin is one of many famous immigrants who have made important contributions to the United States. Berlin left Siberia, Russia, when he was five years old and emigrated to America. During the summer of 1918 he wrote "God Bless America" for a show but then decided it was too serious, and dropped it. Twenty years later, with the threat of war looming in Europe, he dusted it off and revised the lyrics to make the song a tribute to America in peacetime. Kate Smith introduced the revised version of "God Bless America" during a radio broadcast on Armistice Day, 1938 and it soon became an unofficial United States anthem.

Following the attacks of September 11th, 2001, "God Bless America" experienced a surge of patriotic popularity. Representatives of Congress gathered and sang it on the steps of the Capitol. It played when the New York Stock Exchange resumed trading after the attacks. It replaced or accompanied "Take Me Out to the Ballgame" during the seventh-inning stretch at many baseball games. In a sense, it became an anthem of strength and solidarity for that troubled time.

The Library of Congress has the manuscripts and lyrics sheets, and printer's proofs that document the creation of this patriotic song.

TEACHING SUGGESTIONS

➡ Distribute copies of Evaluate That Document! with the sheet music and give students some background information on Berlin and the time in which he wrote "God Bless America." Ask students what the lyrics say about the country in the eyes of this immigrant. Ask students to identify when and where they've heard this classic song and why it might be played on certain occasions at specific events.

➡ Many people feel that "God Bless America" would be a better national anthem than the "Star-Spangled Banner." Ask students to debate the merits of each song. Which would make a better anthem, and why?

➡ The following is a brief list of some famous American immigrants. Ask students to select one and do a brief biography. You could also make a class set of Famous American Immigrant Collector Cards. For example:

Madeline Albright
Isaac Asimov
John James Audubon
Alexander Graham Bell
Irving Berlin
Elizabeth Blackwell
Andrew Carnegie
Albert Einstein
Greta Garbo
Bob Hope
Jacob Riis
Arnold Schwarzenegger

➡ Ask students to list other cultural contributions brought to our country by immigrants, including words in our language, food, celebrations, religion, and other customs.

Oath of Citizenship

Use with pages 38–39.

BACKGROUND

For many immigrants, the moment when they stand and repeat the Oath of Citizenship is the realization of a dream. Prospective citizens have been taking an oath of allegiance to the Constitution since 1790 when the first Naturalization Act was passed. The text shown here is repeated by hundreds of thousands of immigrants each year. Before that happens, though, they must go through the time-consuming process of applying for citizenship. They must also pass a citizenship test, which asks questions about the U.S. Constitution and the nation's history. A sample test shown here was generated by the Department of Justice as practice for would-be citizens. The photograph shows new citizens taking their oaths.

TEACHING SUGGESTIONS

➡ Have students study the Oath of Citizenship and the sample test. Distribute the Evaluate That Document! form (page 17) to help them.

➡ For millions of immigrants the oath ceremony is a moving and wonderful experience. Ask your students to examine the photo on page 39 and consider why this might be a big deal to people? What changes might it cause in their lives? How might it feel to officially sever allegiance to the country that you grew up in? Scary? Liberating?

➡ Ask students to translate the oath into their own words.

➡ Explain to students that people who object to military or civilian service to the government can omit reciting that part of the oath on grounds of "religious training or belief." Are there other parts of the oath that students think people might have trouble with on religious grounds?

➡ Have students find out the steps immigrants must take to become citizens. How long must they live in the U.S.? What are some problems that might disqualify them?

➡ The Immigration and Naturalization Service (INS) maintains a Web site with complete information about the immigration process today. Students can take the complete sample test at that Web site, as well as view statistics and legal requirements. Encourage students to visit: **www.ins.usdoj.gov**.

Who We Are: 2000–Today

Use with pages 40–41.

BACKGROUND

Every four years, the United States conducts a census to gather statistics about our population. Statistics never tell the whole story, and accurate immigration statistics can be particularly elusive. For one thing, illegal immigration is hard to document. For another, numbers don't tell the stories of how and why each immigrant came. However, there is much that we can learn about our population today and the different cultures that shape our nation.

The two pie charts show the region in which U.S. immigrants were born. As the chart reflects, the largest number of immigrants today come from Mexico. The other pie chart shows what types of jobs immigrants hold today. You might want to distribute the Time Line (page 6) and the Immigration Tides graph (page 27) to give context to these snapshots of today.

The photographs on this page tell another part of the story. The bilingual sign, reading "Caution and Prohibido," warns drivers to watch for illegal immigrants fleeing across the Mexico–United States border. Thousands of Mexicans risk their lives every year by crossing the border through dangerous conditions and harsh terrain, hoping to make it into the country illegally. If people do cross safely, they are not guaranteed the right to stay.

The second photograph, taken in 1994, shows Cuban refugees making their way to Key West, Florida aboard crowded and makeshift rafts. When they arrive, they await processing by the U.S. Immigration and Naturalization Service. The line of people in the photograph shown on page 41 are Hutu refugees from Rwanda, waiting in Zaire to be evacuated by the United Nations. The photograph was taken in 1997. Thousands of refugees had fled into the jungles, under attack from Zairian mobs. The U.N. evacuated up to 100 refuges daily, by airlifts.

TEACHING SUGGESTIONS

➼ Use the Evaluate That Document! form (page 17) to explore these documents as primary sources. Explain to your students how the figures are collected. From which world regions do most of our immigrants originate today? Which types of jobs are most common? You can learn more about the U.S. Census, and see more statistics, at **www.census.gov**.

➼ Distribute the Immigration Glossary on page 46 and discuss the meaning of the term refugees. Ask students to write a story using some of the words in the glossary.

➼ Discuss the image shown on the "Caution" sign. What is depicted? What do the basic silhouettes convey? Note the hunched figures, the flying hair and feet of the child, and the general sense of urgency and fleeing.

➼ Ask students to study the expressions on the Cuban refugees' faces. What emotions can they detect? What about the expression and posture of the Hutu refugees? Discuss the United States policy of welcoming refugees from repressive regimes. Encourage students to support an argument for or against this policy.

An American from Iran

Use with pages 42–43.

BACKGROUND

Following the terrorist attacks of September 11, 2001, legislation aimed at protecting our borders also resulted in harsher policies toward immigrants. The U.S. PATRIOT Act was enacted the next month, severely restricting the civil liberties of immigrants. For many Middle Eastern immigrants, the events of 2001 and the ensuing backlash have been particularly painful.

This oral history records the experiences of an Iranian immigrant. Morteza Taherisefat came to the Untied States from Iran in 1978. To his students at Eastside High School in Paterson, N.J., he is known as "Mo" or "Mr. T." He also teaches at the New Jersey Institute of Technology, William Paterson University, and Essex County Community College.

Taherisefat's thoughts reflect the patriotism felt by many immigrants, and the push-and-pull they feel with their old culture.

TEACHING SUGGESTIONS

➼ Distribute copies of Evaluate That Document! (page 17), and have students read the oral history carefully. How does the format of an oral history provide a unique perspective as a primary source? What do they learn from Taherisefat's experiences?

➼ Taherisefat says that he is 99.9% American, and his daughters are 100% American. Discuss what he means by that statement.

➼ The Southern Poverty Law Center has established a program to fight hate and promote tolerance. Students can visit the Web site based on that project: **http://www.tolerance.org.** The Web site includes suggestions about things students can do to promote tolerance.

➼ Encourage your students to become pen pals with someone from another country: **http://dir.yahoo.com/Social_Science/ Communications/Writing/Correspondence/ Pen_Pals/Children/** (Make sure students obtain permission from their parents to participate in the pen pal project.)

Evaluate That Document!

Title or name of document _____

Date of document _____

Type of document:

❏ letter   ❏ patent

❏ diary/journal   ❏ poster

❏ newspaper article   ❏ advertisement

❏ photograph   ❏ drawing/painting

❏ map   ❏ cartoon

❏ telegram   ❏ other _____

Point of view:

Who created this document? _____

For whom was this document created? _____

_____

What was the purpose for creating this document? _____

_____

What might the person who created it have been trying to express? _____

_____

What are two things you can learn about the time period from this primary source?

_____

_____

What other questions do you have about this source?

_____

_____

_____

_____

_____

_____

THE POTATO FAMINE
1845

IRISH EMIGRANTS LEAVING HOME.—THE PRIEST'S BLESSING.

The Granger Collection

The Eviction

"June 16, [*1847*]: The past night was very rough, and I enjoyed little rest. No additional cases of sickness were reported, but there were signs of insubordination amongst the healthy men who complained of starvation and want of water for their sick wives and children. A deputation [*group*] came aft to acquaint the captain with their grievances, but he ordered them away, and would not listen to a word from them. When he went below, the ringleaders threatened that they would break into the provision store. . . . In order to make a deeper impression on their minds, [*the captain*] brought out the old blunderbuss [*a type of rifle*] from which he fired a shot [*in the air*]. . . . The deputation slunk away muttering complaints. If they were resolute they could easily have seized upon the provisions."

Robert Whyte, *The Ocean Plague: A Voyage to Quebec in an Irish Immigrant Vessel*, 1848

THE POTATO FAMINE

1845

English landowners used extreme methods to force Irish tenants from their homes, including battering rams, as shown in this photograph.

"25th November [1850]: Another child, making about 12 in all, died of dysentery from want of proper nourishing food, and was thrown into the sea sown up, along with a great stone, in a cloth. No funeral service has yet been performed, the doctor informs me, over any one who has died on board; the Catholics objecting, as he says, to the performance of any such service by a layman [someone who is not a priest]. . . .

"3rd December: A few of the passengers were taken ashore to the Hospital at Staten Island, and we arrived alongside the quay at New York this afternoon. The 900 passengers dispersed as usual among the various fleecing houses [shady places that bilked money from immigrants], to be partially or entirely disabled for pursuing their travels into the interior in search of employment.

—Letter from Vere Foster to Lord Hobart, December 1850

LURE OF THE LAND
Late 1800s

LURE OF THE LAND
1869

WHERE TO EMIGRATE. AND WHY.

FREDERICK B. GODDARD.

THE GOLD RUSH
1849

Getty Images

In school we did not study geography. We had only the venerable classics to commit to memory. So the outside world was just a vague notion in my mind, and, for that reason, all the more fascinating. Once a cousin ... returned from Chinshan, the "Gold Mountain," and told us strange tales of men becoming tremendously rich overnight by finding gold in river beds. To this day, San Francisco is known among our people as the "Old Gold Mountain." Once I was very sick, and in my delirium, so mother told me, I talked of nothing but wanting to go to Chinshan.

Huie Ngou, Huie Yao, Huie Lin and I were good chums as well as cousins. We studied in the same village school, played shuttlecock on the village green, and spent long days together in the foothills with our cows. We told each other our woes and joys, and concocted ambitious exploits, one of which was to go together across the great sea to that magic land where gold was to be had free from river beds and men became rich overnight. ...

We knew what poverty meant. To toil and sweat year in and year out, as our parents did, and to get nowhere; to be sick and burn or shiver with chills without a doctor's care; always to wear rough homespun; going without shoes, even on cold winter days; without books or time to read them—that was the common tale of rural life, as I knew it.

—Huie Kin describing his decision to leave China in 1865

Scholastic Professional Books

THE MAGIC WASHER

1886

To Whom it may Concern: This is a Liquid Washing Compound, and is FULLY GUARANTEED BETTER THAN ANYTHING EVER OFFERED TO THE PUBLIC; its constant use will not injure the cloths nor turn them yellow. For sale by the Gallon, Half-gallon and Quart. TRY A SAMPLE AND BE SURPRISED.

We have no use for them since we got this WONDERFUL WASHER: What a blessing to tired mothers: It costs so little and don't injure the clothes.

23

AMERICA FEVER

Settlers in Swede Lake, MN 1896

Memoir of Andreas Ueland

Father died in January, 1870. That changed abruptly my whole aspect of life. An older brother was to have the farm after Mother; what was I to do? Mother wished to have me educated to teach, but I did not wish to be a teacher. There was left the choice to stay home and wait for something to turn up, go out as a laborer or to learn a trade, or to sea, or to America!

A farmer from Houston County, Minnesota, returned on a visit the winter of '70–'71. He infected half the population in that district with what was called the America fever, and I who was then the most susceptible caught the fever in its most virulent form. No more amusement of any kind, only brooding on how to get away to America. It was like a desperate case of homesickness reversed. Mother was appealed to with all the arguments I could think of, such as that I would escape being drafted as a soldier and would surely soon return. On my solemn promise to be back within five years, she consented, stocked me up with many new clothes, and with a feather quilt to keep warm nights, and with a little money in addition to the $93 inherited from Father, so that, all in all, I started equipped as well as the boy of the tale who left his home for great adventures with "horse, hound and hundred dollars."

—Andreas Ueland, excerpt from *Recollections of an Immigrant,* 1929

AMERICA FEVER

Letter to Sweden

. . . Much I have seen, heard, and experienced, but nothing unhappy, no shady sides. To be sure I believed when I departed from home, from the fatherland, from family, friends, and acquaintances, that everything would at first be rather unfamiliar. But no, strangely enough, everything is as I wished it should be. The country is beautiful, if any land on earth deserves to be called so. And if you compare conditions here with Sweden's, there is no similarity at all. The soil consists of a kind of dark loam over a layer of marl on a clay base; your finest plowlands at home cannot compare with the rich prairies here, where golden harvests grow from year to year without having to be manured or ditched. No stones, no stumps hinder the cultivator's plow. If you add to this that one can almost get such land as a gift or for an insignificant sum compared with its natural value, you soon have an idea WHY America IS truly and undeniably better than old Sweden. But here is another thing, taxes do not consume the American farmer, they are extremely light. America maintains no EXPENSIVE royal house, no inactive armies, which undermine the people's welfare; such things are considered here as superfluous articles and EXTREMELY harmful. Never has a freer people trodden, cultivated, and tended a better land than this. Hundreds of thousands of persons have found here the happiness they vainly sought in Europe's lands. . . . The climate is remarkably fine; nothing stands in our way except the language. We cannot understand their speech, but it is possible for us to learn as well as others have done. I see after this first short time that it is going well. And therefore you can understand that I do not regret the journey, other than to regret that I had not made it before. But better late than never, as the saying goes, and I agree.

—C.F. Carlsson, Clarksville, Merrick Co., Nebraska, early 1880s

"ONLY AN EMIGRANT"
1879

ONLY AN EMIGRANT (song lyrics)

Only an emigrant! Son of the soil,
With my hands ready for labor and toil,
Willing for anything honest I be,
Surely there's room on the prairies for me . . .

IMMIGRATION TIDES

1800–2000

AMI—National Park Service

Immigrants on the *Atlantic Liner*, 1906

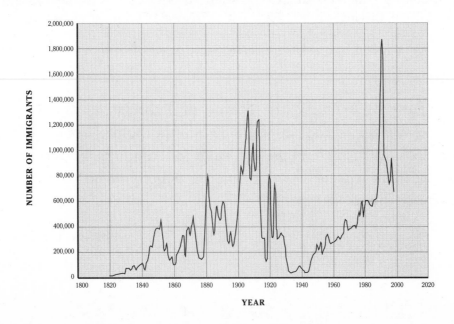

27

THE STATUE OF LIBERTY

NEW YORK–WELCOME TO THE LAND OF **FREEDOM**– AN OCEAN STEAMER PASSING
THE STATUE OF LIBERTY–SCENE ON THE STEERAGE DECK [original caption]

Engraving printed in *Frank Leslie's Illustrated Newspaper*, July 2, 1887

The first time I saw the Statue of Liberty all the
people were rushing to the side of the boat. "Look at
her, look at her," and in all kinds of tongues. "There
she is, there she is!" like it was somebody who was
greeting them.

—Elizabeth Phillips, Irish immigrant

Library of Congress

Scholastic Professional Books

THE STATUE OF LIBERTY

The New Colossus

Not like the brazen giant of Greek fame,
With conquering limbs astride from land to land;
Here at our sea-washed, sunset gates shall stand
A mighty woman with a torch, whose flame
Is the imprisoned lightning, and her name
Mother of Exiles. From her beacon-hand
Glows world-wide welcome; her mild eyes command
The air-bridged harbor that twin cities frame.

"Keep, ancient lands, your storied pomp!" cries she
With silent lips. "Give me your tired, your poor,
Your huddled masses yearning to breathe free,
The wretched refuse of your teeming shore.
Send these, the homeless, tempest-tost to me.
I lift my lamp beside the golden door."

—Emma Lazarus, 1883

"What Happened to the One We Used to Have?"
1946 editorial cartoon from *The Washington Post*

ELLIS ISLAND

Library of Congress

Ellis Island, 1905

Passport of a Greek immigrant, 1916.

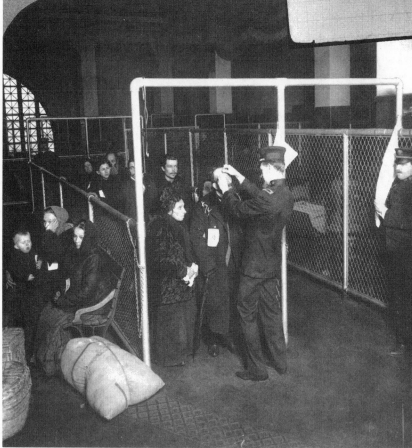

When they discovered health problems, inspectors wrote letters in chalk on the clothing of new arrivals to flag the attention of other agents. If the disease were serious, immigration officials might refuse the immigrant permission to enter the country. Here are a few of the marks they used:

X	Suspected mental problem
⊗	Mental disease
B	Back
C	Conjunctivitis
Ft	Feet
H	Heart
P	Physical & Lungs
Pg	Pregnancy
Sc	Scalp
S	Senility

Eye exam at Ellis Island, 1913

 Library of Congress

ELLIS ISLAND

Contract Ticket No._____

Questions required by the United States Government to be answered by the Immigrants before Booking.

CUNARD LINE.
NOTICE.

If it is found upon the arrival of the immigrant in the United States that the following questions have not been correctly answered, the immigrant will be immediately returned.

The immigrant will be required to swear to the truth of the following answers, if it be called for by the Commissioner of Immigration at the Port of Arrival in the United States. (A false oath will subject the immigrant to fine or imprisonment.)

Name_____ Date when booked_____

Agent's Name_____ Agent's Place of Business_____

Name of Steamer for which Booked_____ Date of sailing from_____

1. No. on List_____
2. Name in full_____
   (In cases of families or parties, the particulars of names and ages may be written on the back of this form.)
3. Age_____ Years,_____ Months.
4. Sex_____
5. Married or Single_____
6. Calling or occupation_____
7. Able to Read and Write_____
8. Nationality (country owning political allegiance or of which citizen or subject)_____
9. *Race or people_____
10. Last Residence—Province, City or Town (Address in full, and how long resident there)_____

11. Final destination, if any, beyond port of landing (State, City or Town)_____
12. Whether having a ticket to such final destination_____
13. By whom was passage paid_____
14. Whether in possession of $50, and if less, how much_____
15. Whether ever before in the United States, and if so { When_____ / Where_____
16. Whether going to join a relative or friend, and if so, what relative or friend— his name and complete address_____
17. Ever in Prison or Almshouse or Institution for care and treatment of the Insane, or supported by charity, if so, which_____
18. Whether a Polygamist_____
19. Whether an Anarchist_____
20. Whether coming by reason of any offer, solicitation, promise, or agreement, express or implied, to labor in the United States_____
21. Condition of Health, Mental and Physical_____
22. Deformed or Crippled, Nature, Length of time and Cause_____
23. If of other than British Nationality, and already residing in the United Kingdom—state original port of arrival in the United Kingdom_____
24. **Personal Description.**—Height_____ feet_____ inches.
    Complexion_____ Colour of hair_____ Colour of Eyes_____
    Marks of Identification_____
25. **Place of birth**_____

I hereby certify that I have made true answers to the questions which were asked in language understood by me and which answers have been recorded above.

(Sign here)

☞ "Race or People" is to be determined by the stock from which they sprang and the language they speak. List of races will be found on back of this sheet. ☜

P.T.O.

Questionnaire used by the Cunard Line to prescreen immigrants.   National Archives

ANGEL ISLAND
1910–1940

Four days after the Qiquao Festival,
I boarded the steamship for America.
Time flew like a shooting arrow.
Already, a cool autumn has passed.
Counting on my fingers, several months have elapsed.
Still I am at the beginning of the road.
My heart is nervous with anticipation.

—Author unknown

Chinese boys lined up for medical
examination, c. 1910

I am distressed that we Chinese are
in this wooden building
It is actually racial barriers which cause
difficulties on Yingtai Island.
Even while they are tyrannical they still
claim to be humanitarian.
I should regret my taking the risks of
coming in the first place.

—Author unknown

This is a message to those who live here not
to worry excessively.
Instead, you must cast your idle worries to
the flowing stream.
Experiencing a little ordeal is not hardship.
Napoleon was once a prisoner on an island.

—Author unknown

AT HOME, AT WORK, AT PLAY

early 1900s

Library of Congress

Immigrant family sewing at home, 1915 (Lewis Hine)

Library of Congress

Street vendors in New York City, 1915 (Lewis Hine)

LIFE IN AMERICA
early 1900s

At Left:
Unauthorized immigration lodgings in a Bayard Street tenement in New York City c. 1890 (Jacob Riis)

Below:
Playground in tenement alley, Boston, 1909 (Lewis Hine)

Library of Congress

Library of Congress

BECOMING AN AMERICAN

early 1900s

GRANITE CITY
AMERICANIZATION SCHOOLS

Monday
and
Thursday
Evenings
7:30 p. m.

Beginning
Monday,
September
the 27th,
1920

Underwood & Underwood

These two men are brothers, one is an American Citizen and the other has just come to this country with their old mother. See the difference in the way they dress and look. America is a great country. In America everybody has a chance. Everybody who comes to America from the old country ought to learn the American language and become an American citizen. If the people that come to America do not become Americans, this country will soon be like the old country.

SCHOOLS:

HIGH SCHOOL, 20TH AND D STREETS
LINCOLN PLACE, 917 PACIFIC AVENUE

LIBERTY SCHOOL, 20TH AND O STREETS
MADISON SCHOOL, 1322 MADISON AVENUE

Keep America Great.   Become an American Citizen   **Learn The Language.**

Press-Record Publishing Co.   1534 D St., Granite City, Ill

National Archives

Broadside prodding adult arrivals to come to school so that they can become more American in language, dress, and attitude.

National Geographic Image Collection

Adults learning English in a classroom, and simultaneously being given a lesson in good grooming.

BECOMING AN AMERICAN
early 1900s

National Geographic Image Collection

A teacher "preparing breakfast."

Don't Bite the Hand That's Feeding You

If you don't like your Uncle Sammy,
Then go back to your home or the sea,
To the land from where you came
Whatever be your name
But don't be ungrateful to me,
If you don't like the stars in old Glory,
If you don't like the red, white, and blue
Then don't act like the cur in the story
Don't bite the hand that's feeding you.

c. 1917

Scholastic Professional Books

GOD BLESS AMERICA

Spoken introduction:
While the storm clouds gather far across the sea,
Let us swear allegiance to a land that's free,
Let us all be grateful for a land so fair,
As we raise our voices in a solemn prayer.

The Estate of Irving Berlin

Lyrics:

God Bless America,
Land that I love.
Stand beside her, and guide her
Thru the night with a light from above.

From the mountains, to the prairies,
To the oceans, white with foam
God bless America,
My home sweet home.

Oath of Citizenship

"I hereby declare, on oath, that I absolutely and entirely renounce and abjure all allegiance and fidelity to any foreign prince, potentate, state, or sovereignty, of whom or which I have heretofore been a subject or citizen; that I will support and defend the Constitution and laws of the United States of America against all enemies, foreign and domestic; that I will bear true faith and allegiance to the same; that I will bear arms on behalf of the United States when required by the law; that I will perform noncombatant service in the Armed Forces of the United States when required by the law; that I will perform work of national importance under civilian direction when required by the law; and that I take this obligation freely without any mental reservation or purpose of evasion; so help me God. In acknowledgment whereof I have hereunto affixed my signature."

(Present-day Oath of Citizenship; first oath developed in 1790)

A 1976 bicentennial naturalization ceremony held onboard the U.S.S. *Constitution*

UPI/Corbis

Scholastic Professional Books

INS Citizenship Test

(from 100 sample questions, first 25)

1. What are the colors of our flag?

2. How many stars are there in our flag?

3. What color are the stars on our flag?

4. What do the stars on the flag mean?

5. How many stripes are there in the flag?

6. What color are the stripes?

7. What do the stripes on the flag mean?

8. How many states are there in the Union?

9. What is the 4th of July?

10. What is the date of Independence Day?

11. Independence from whom?

12. What country did we fight during the Revolutionary War?

13. Who was the first President of the United States?

14. Who is the president of the United States today?

15. Who is the vice-president of the United States today?

16. Who elects the president of the United States?

17. Who becomes president of the United States if the president should die?

18. For how long do we elect the president?

19. What is the Constitution?

20. Can the Constitution be changed?

21. What do we call a change to the Constitution?

22. How many changes or amendments are there to the Constitution?

23. How many branches are there in our government?

24. What are the three branches of our government?

25. What is the legislative branch of our government?

WHO WE ARE

Immigrants' Country of Origin: 2000

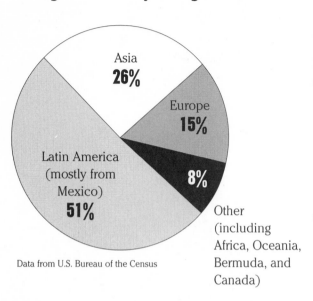

Asia
26%

Europe
15%

Latin America
(mostly from
Mexico)
51%

8%

Other
(including
Africa, Oceania,
Bermuda, and
Canada)

Data from U.S. Bureau of the Census

Steve Rubin/The Image Works

This bilingual sign warns drivers near San Diego, California, to watch for illegal immigrants crossing the Mexican border.

Reuters New Media/Corbis

Taken in 1994, this photograph shows refugees from Cuba arriving off the coast of Key West, Florida, in makeshift rafts.

WHO WE ARE

Immigrant Jobs: 2000

Farming, forestry, and fishing

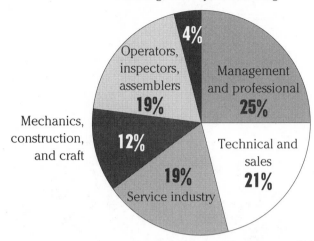

Operators, inspectors, assemblers
19%

Management and professional
25%

Mechanics, construction, and craft

12%

19%
Service industry

Technical and sales
21%

4%

Data from U.S. Bureau of the Census

AP/Wide World Photos

This photograph, taken in 1997, shows Hutu refugees from Rwanda lined up in Zaire, waiting for a United Nations airlift.

AN AMERICAN FROM IRAN
2002

This oral history records the experiences of an Iranian immigrant. Morteza Taherisefat came to the Untied States from Iran in 1978. To his students at Eastside High School in Paterson, N.J., he is known as "Mo" or "Mr. T." He also teaches at the New Jersey Institute of Technology, William Paterson University, and Essex County Community College.

Taherisefat's thoughts reflect the patriotism felt by many immigrants, and the push-and-pull they feel with their old culture.

Morteza Taherisefat and his family

Interview

I grew up in Teheran, the capital of Iran. I come from a very big family. When I was 21, I left all of them to come to the United States, to follow the sunlight, to follow a dream. I came alone, with just one cousin in America.

Now I have a wife and two daughters and a nice home and job. My fourth-grade daughter just did a report for school about Ellis Island. I didn't come by a boat to Ellis Island. I came by Pan Am, to JFK.

When I landed I was shocked, excited, amazed. Even though Teheran is the capital of Iran, we had no buildings with one hundred floors. Nothing comparable. So I was just amazed looking around.

I was supposed to fill out some forms, but I spoke no English or only very broken English. I couldn't even read or write my name! Finally someone else in the line behind me from Iran said I needed help and I waited an hour, and then finally someone came who could translate for me. A cousin of mine who lived in the Bronx came and picked me up.

I stayed with him for two weeks, but then

I moved to Jersey City to begin the dream. I worked in every job you can imagine. I cleaned floors, sold newspapers, cleaned bathrooms, sold ice cream – you name it, I did it. And I went to school: I studied electronics and mathematics and digital signal processing. And now I'm getting a Certificate of Supervision, and I'm going to be the head of my department.

After I was here a few years I called my family and said, "I need a wife." And they found someone for me, and after a few phone calls, my father married us over the phone. A few months later we met for the first time, in Istanbul – and we were already married. Fortunately, she was very beautiful! It took a long time to get her over here, several years and we kept having visits in Turkey.

Now my whole family are citizens. Taking the Oath of Citizenship, that was a very good moment. We are very proud citizens. I am an American. I am 99.9% American. My daughters are 100% American, but they know where they came from. My daughter went to my homeland twice with my wife. I didn't go with them, because I was afraid. I was afraid that my country would say, "What are you doing here? Are you a terrorist?"

But then last year my father called me and told me that if I wanted to ever see him I'd better come because he didn't know how much longer he's going to be around. So after 23 ½ years, I saw my family for the first time. I was afraid to go to Iran so we met in Damascus – my father and eight of my family members. My sister was 37 when I left, and when I saw her she was in her 60s, with gray hair. I went to meet my closest brother at the airport. He's just 1 ½ years older than I am, so [as children] we played all the time. And now I didn't know how I was going to recognize him at the airport, 24 years later. I looked around to see if I could see my

brother, and then I saw someone who looked just like my little girl. I asked, are you my brother? And we both were crying. It was very emotional. It was wonderful to see everyone, but also strange. I'm not part of them. I'm totally western. After the one week together I told them, I said, I love you guys. And I'm sorry if I'm not loveable. I tried to be very careful to watch my mouth and not say anything that was not respectful.

I was born Muslim, but I don't go to a mosque. I practice my religion: be kind; be helpful to others; be respectful. That's my religion. I believe that black, white, Jewish, Islamic, Catholic, we all live under one roof, and whether it's God or Allah, or Yahweh, or whatever you want to believe, we all belong to the same Creator.

My mother-in-law was visiting us on September 11th. We were all so horrified. Afterwards, she was afraid to go out in our neighborhood with her head covering on. She was afraid people would be angry or hurt her. We told her, no, it's o.k. But for a while she wouldn't go out.

After September 11th, I just feel even more strongly: I am an American. Like all Americans, I have so much sympathy for these innocent people. The only thing we can do is pray. And give to charity. And as Americans we have to move on and live our lives, not let the terrorists have a free shot. Not just sit there and wait for them, like they want. If I want to take a plane, I'll take a plane. Or go to a shopping mall or a baseball game, because if we don't they will succeed. If we don't move on, then they have destroyed our lives, and we can't let that happen.

—Morteza Taherisefat,
from an interview with Karen Baicker, 2002

U.S. IMMIGRATION KWL CHART

In the KWL chart below, write down what you already know about the United States immigration in the *K* space, and then write what you want to learn in the *W* space. When you've found the answers to your questions, record your discoveries in the "What I learned" section (*L* space) and new questions in the "What I still want to learn" section.

What I Know

_____

_____

_____

_____

_____

_____

What I Want to know

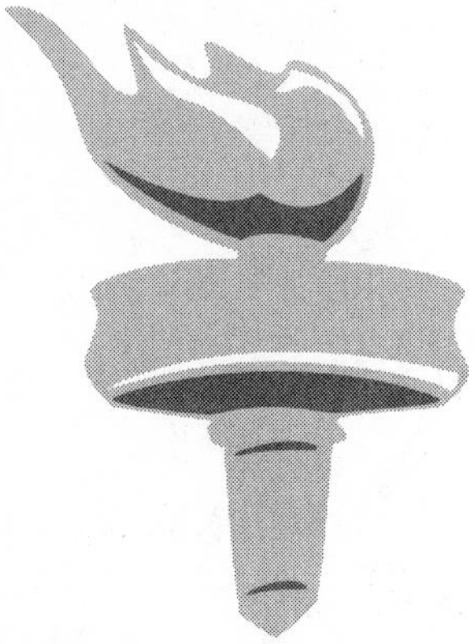

_____

_____

_____

_____

_____

What I Learned

_____

_____

_____

_____

_____

What I Still want to learn

_____

_____

_____

_____

_____

IMMIGRATION MAP: 1800-2000

Use this map to determine when immigrants came from different countries.

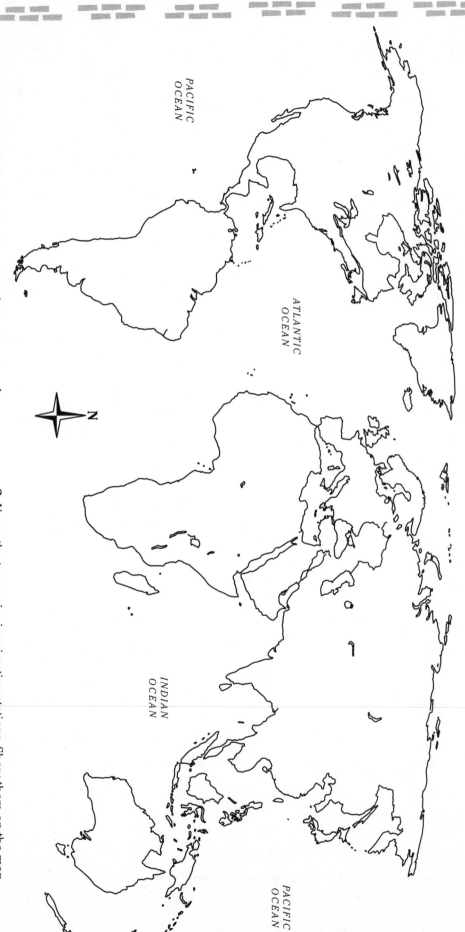

PACIFIC OCEAN

ATLANTIC OCEAN

INDIAN OCEAN

PACIFIC OCEAN

N

1. In 1840, the failure of a certain crop caused a great wave of immigration. What was the crop? Where did the immigrants come from? Show their route on the map with an arrow.

2. In 1885, the United States received a gift from another country. What was that gift? Color the country that gave the gift green. Make a green "X" to show where the gift is located.

3. Name the two major immigration stations. Show them on the map with blue dots, and write the years that they were open for active immigration stations.

4. Between 1820 and 1996, what three countries provided the most immigrants to the U.S. Show them on the map with red "S" ("source"). In 1996, what were the top three countries. Show them on the map with green "S".

Immigration Glossary

No Comprendé? Here are some terms you can use when you write about immigrants' experiences in their new country.

assimilate
to adapt to a new country

citizen
a person living as a legal resident of a country or place, entitled by birth or naturalization to the protection of that place (In the United States, some citizens are born here with automatic citizenship; others become citizens through a legal process of immigration.)

deport
to expel from a country

emigration
the act of leaving one's country to settle in another

immigration
the act of coming to a foreign country to live

naturalize
to allow a foreign person to become a citizen

Old Country
the native country of an immigrant. For many immigrants in the 1880s–1920s, Eastern Europe was the Old Country

quota
a ceiling on the number of people allowed to enter the country

refugee
immigrant who flees his or her country because of persecution, war, or such disasters as famines or epidemics (Refugees are also known as displaced persons, or DPs.)

resident
someone living legally in this country who is not a citizen

visa
a permit that allows a non-citizen to stay in another country on a temporary basis

Story Starter Tip!

If you choose to write a story about the experiences of an immigrant here are some suggestions to get you started:

*I stared at the empty trunk, studying the block of space. That space would soon contain my only possessions in the world.

*There it was! In front of my eyes. I blinked to make sure but there could be no doubt. Standing tall and proud against the sky was Lady Liberty. We had arrived.

*Thirty-seven dollars and fifty cents. That's what I had left after the expenses of the journey. How was I supposed to get the train to Chicago?

*I had my best outfit on and shined my shoes. But somehow it all seemed wrong as I stepped into the halls of my new school.

*I've learned so much English since we came here. But my mother still knows only a few words. So now I translate for her. And that can get me into trouble . . .

IMMIGRATION JOURNAL

IMMIGRATION MAP ANSWER KEY

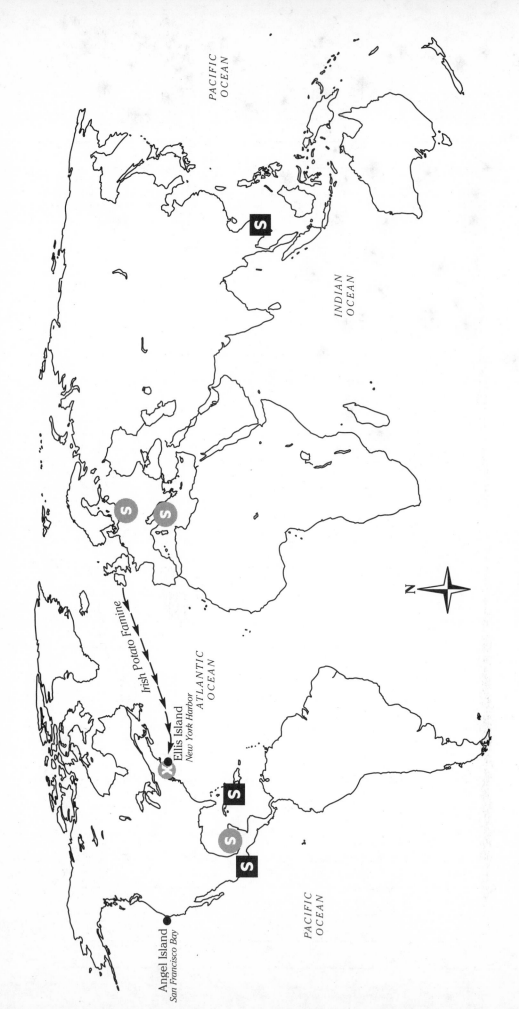

1. Potato (*crop failure*); Ireland (*source of immigrants of the potato famine*); an arrow should be drawn from Ireland to New York.

2. The Statue of Liberty; France; a green "X" should mark New York Harbor.

3. Students should mark with a blue dot and label Ellis Island, in New York harbor (1892–1954) and Angel Island in the San Francisco Bay (1910–1940).

4. Germany, Mexico, and Italy should be labeled with a red "S" **S** . Mexico, Cuba, and Vietnam should be labeled with a green "S" **S** .